ON THE MAP

CHINA

Titles in this Series:

Canada	Japan
China	Mexico
Egypt	Russia
France	Spain
Germany	U.S.A.
Italy	West Indies

Design: M&M partnership
Electronic production: Scott Melcer
Photographs: ZEFA
Map artwork: Raymond Turvey
Cover photo: Schoolchildren exercising

Library of Congress Cataloging-in-Publication Data

Flint, David, 1946–
    China / David Flint
        p.   cm. — (On the map)
    Includes bibliographical references and index.
    Summary: An illustrated introduction to the geography, people, family life, food, sports, industry, and famous landmarks of China.
    ISBN 0–8114–3421–4
    1. China — Juvenile literature.   [1. China.]   I. Title.
II. Series.
DS706.F57   1994
951–dc20   93–15794
                                                                CIP
                                                                 AC

Printed and bound in the United States.
1 2 3 4 5 6 7 8 9 0 VH 98 97 96 95 94 93

CHINA

David Flint

RSVP

RAINTREE
STECK-VAUGHN
PUBLISHERS
The Steck-Vaughn Company

Austin, Texas

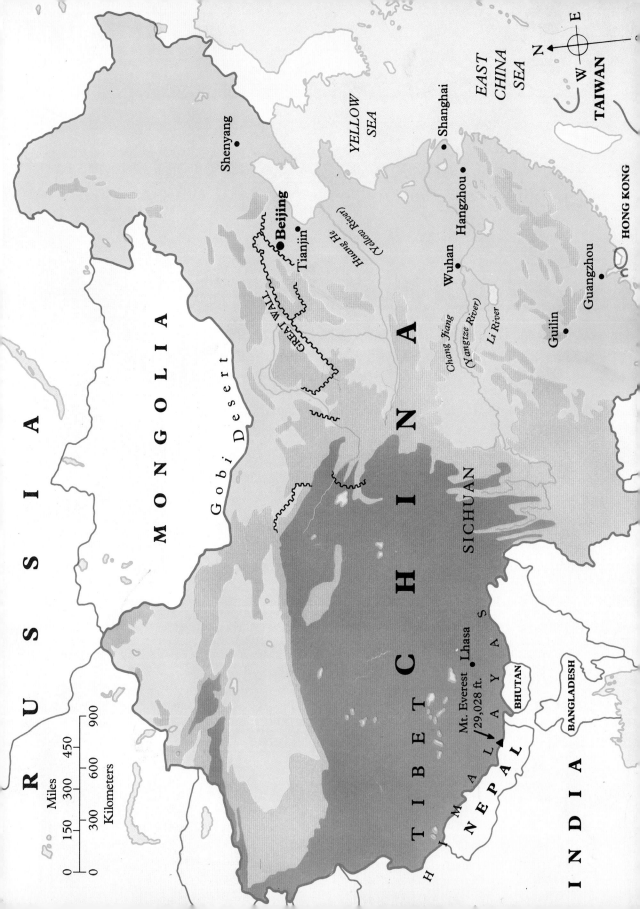

Contents

Tourists sail the Li River to see
towering limestone hills near
Guilin, in southern China.

Shanghai, on the east coast, is China's
main port. It is a modern city.

In western China, villages cling
to hilltops high in the clouds.

A Large Asian Country

The People's Republic of China is a huge country on the continent of Asia. In area, China is the third largest country in the world. It is just a little larger than the United States.

China is bordered by 14 countries, including India on the west, Mongolia and Russia on the north, and Vietnam and Laos on the south. If you look at the map opposite the Contents page, you can find the other countries that border China. You will also see that China has a long coastline on the east. It borders the South China, East China, and Yellow seas.

In population, China is the largest country in the world. More than 1 billion people live there. Think of it this way. One out of every five people in the world lives in China.

Most people in China belong to the group called Han Chinese. The Han Chinese live primarily in eastern China, the most densely populated area of the country. The native language of the Han people is a form of Chinese. Five percent of the people in China belong to minority groups, who tend to live in less crowded, and often more rugged, areas of the country. Their native languages and traditional life-styles are different from that of other Chinese.

Land of Contrasts

China has many kinds of landforms and climates. Mountains, deserts, and plateaus make up the dry, western part of the country.

The Himalayan mountain chain and the Tibetan Plateau are in southwestern China. Mount Everest, which is usually considered the world's highest mountain peak, is in the Himalayas. The Tibetan Plateau is north of the Himalayas. This plateau of flat, high land is often called the roof of the world. The weather on the plateau is bitterly cold for most of the year. This is the home of the Tibetan people. Most of them are farmers or yak herders. Yaks are large, long-haired animals that look somewhat like oxen. They are used as pack animals, for farm work.

The Gobi Desert is a large dry area in northwestern China. Camels, oases, and huge sand dunes are found on the desert, which is surrounded by mountains. The Gobi is very hot in summer and extremely cold in winter.

Hills, plains, and river valleys make up much of eastern China. Farmers grow wheat in the north and rice in the south. The northeast, though quite dry, has excellent soil. Summers in the northeast are hot, and winters are long and very cold.

China has vast deserts. Few plants grow in this northwestern desert because it is so dry.

On the plains of eastern China, small rice fields are separated by footpaths.

Mount Everest—the highest mountain in the world, at 29,028 feet.

Along the Rivers

China has two great rivers. The Huang He, or Yellow River, flows from central China to the Yellow Sea. The river is 2,903 miles long, from its source to its mouth. It is the sixth longest river in the world.

The Huang He is important to farming. It carries good soil, which builds up on the bottom of the river. When the Huang He changes its course, which it sometimes does, the old river bottom becomes good farmland. In the past, millions of people lost their lives when the Huang He flooded. The river was sometimes known as China's Sorrow. Now, the banks have been raised to prevent destructive flooding.

The Chang Jiang, sometimes called the Yangtze River, runs south of the Huang He. The Chang Jiang also begins in central China. It winds through several deep gorges and continues eastward until it reaches the East China Sea near Shanghai. The Chang Jiang is at least 3,434 miles long and is the third longest river in the world. Chang Jiang means "Long River."

Many crops are grown along the Chang Jiang, including rice, the most important crop in China. The Chang Jiang is an important transportation route, even for oceangoing ships.

This bridge across the Chang Jiang (Yangtze River) was built between 1955 and 1957 at Wuhan. Wuhan is an important center of industry and commerce.

Cormorants are used for fishing in many Chinese rivers. These birds dive to catch fish. Bands around their throats stop them from swallowing the fish.

Tiananmen Square is in the heart of Beijing. Here huge parades are held. In 1989 about 1 million people gathered to demand more freedom from the government..

Even in the Old City, there are modern services such as telephones.

The television station in Beijing show China's more modern architecture.

Beijing, Capital of China

Beijing, sometimes called Peking, has been the capital of China off and on for thousands of years. Today Beijing is the center of Chinese government, industry, education, and transportation. The city has many things to see and do. Although ticket lines may be long, Beijing residents can go out to enjoy opera, ballet, theater, and movies. They can visit libraries, museums, and a famous zoo.

Beijing is China's second largest city. It is part of a district with more than 9 million people. The central city, called the Old City, has many old houses in an area bordering narrow tree-lined alleys. The suburbs are built up with factories and apartment buildings. The district of Beijing even includes farms, where crops and animals are raised, and products such as baskets and furniture are made.

The Forbidden City is in the Old City. Chinese emperors once lived there in gold-roofed palaces surrounded by beautiful gardens. During the time of the emperors, ordinary people were not allowed inside the Forbidden City. Today the palaces and parks are open to all.

Beijing is crowded with people, but there is little automobile traffic. Most people ride bicycles.

Family Life

The family, not the individual, is the basic unit of society in China. Old people are highly respected within the family and the society. Chinese families often include grandparents, a grown-up son, and his wife and child. Most parents work outside the home, and grandparents, especially grandmothers, take care of the home and child.

The Chinese government encourages parents to have only one child. The idea is to slow down and eventually stop population growth. Otherwise, the government fears there will not be enough land and food to go around for everyone.

Most families live in rural areas, in farm villages or small towns. A rural family is most likely to live in a house made of brick or stone. However, there are many other kinds of houses in rural China, built to suit the land, climate, and way of life. In some places, cave houses have been built into cliffs. In others, desert nomads transport their sturdy tents, called yurts, from place to place.

City families usually have less living space than farm families. A city family may live in a tiny house or in an apartment with two or three rooms. Often a bathroom or kitchen is shared with another family.

China has a shortage of apartments. Many rooms, such as this one in Sichuan, serve as both living room and bedroom.

Grandparents, like this grandmother in Tibet, often look after children while their parents are at work.

New apartments in Guilin. Apartment buildings usually have stores and often a health clinic nearby.

In summer this village barber works outside on the sidewalk, where it is cooler.

Food is sold at booths like this one at a market in Beijing. Rice is the main part of the meal with fish or meat and lots of vegetables.

Chinese food is colorful and delicious. People eat with chopsticks instead of knives and forks.

Food

Grain is the basic food of China. In northern China people eat noodles or bread made from grain. In southern China, rice is more common. Thousands of kinds of rice are raised and eaten in China.

A proper diet has always been a part of being Chinese. Everyday meals include fan, which is grain, and cai, which is any food cut into bite-sized pieces. Cai is usually vegetables, perhaps with bits of chicken, pork, or seafood. A family may get along with very little cai, but plenty of fan is essential.

Food is usually steamed or stir-fried in a wok, or bowl-shaped cooking pan. Meals are eaten with chopsticks and spoons—knives stay in the kitchen. It is not uncommon for people to eat outdoors in good weather.

Meals usually begin and end with tea. Boiled water or beer may be taken with the food. Ordinary meals do not include dessert; they often end with soup.

The banquet is an important type of recreation in China. A banquet is not grain based. It might include roast duck, fried whole fish, stir-fried meat and vegetables, and other foods prepared and served in an elegant way.

Going to School

For much of Chinese history, most people could not read or write. However, learning was respected. Today most people in China can read and write. After the communists took over the country in 1949, they set up schools for adults and made laws requiring children to attend elementary school.

Many children today also go to nursery school. At these schools, run by the factories, offices, or farms where their parents work, children are taught to cooperate and share. At age six or seven they begin elementary school. Five and one-half days a week, school begins at 8 A.M. and ends at 4 P.M. Often the whole school exercises together before lessons start.

Students must spend a long time learning to read and write. Written Chinese does not have an alphabet with letters that stand for sounds. Instead, children must memorize how to write thousands of characters, each one with its own meaning.

Between age 11 and 15, some students go to middle school. If they pass certain exams, they may go on to a college or university. However, most young people go to work after elementary or middle school. Further education and training are available at many work sites.

Even very young children are regularly taken on school field trips.
This group is visiting the Imperial Palace in Beijing.

Most children begin elementary school when they are six or seven years old.
There are many children in China, and schools often seem overcrowded.

Getting Around

Most people in China get around by bicycle. Very few people own cars. In towns, roads are divided into two lanes, one for bicycles and one for trucks and buses. In rural areas, people usually walk. In parts of the countryside, depending upon the landscape, people still use horses, mules, donkeys, camels, or yaks to carry themselves and their goods.

Transportation over long distances has been a problem in China because of the vastness of the country and the varied and often rugged landscape. People take buses for relatively short trips and trains for longer trips. Trains, though cheap, are usually full. A person might have to stand in several different lines before getting on. Trucks are often used to carry people and goods to remote areas where trains do not go.

China has more than 100 airports. However, air travel is expensive. Chinese officials and foreign tourists are the main people who use it.

Rivers and canals carry most of the heavy goods in China. Since most of the rivers run west to east, they are linked by canals that run north and south. The Grand Canal is the longest and oldest waterway built by humans. Parts of it are still used today.

Boats called junks carry goods along the rivers. Families sometimes live on board.

Camels are still used in this desert in northwestern China.

In cities like Shanghai, there are trolleybuses and taxis.

Most people take a train when they go on a long trip.

Board games are often played outdoors, where they attract lots of spectators.

Many people appreciate the beautiful costumes of Chinese theater.

These people are exercising before they begin work. They believe the exercise is good for them and helps them concentrate.

Sports, Leisure, and Special Days

Chinese people have little indoor living space, and they spend lots of time outdoors. Even in the early morning in cities and towns, many people go to parks to practice tai chi, or shadowboxing.

Table tennis, badminton, volleyball, and basketball are all popular outdoor sports. Basketball nets and table tennis tables can be found outside most factories, offices, schools, apartment buildings, and in parks. Chess and card games are popular pastimes that are often pursued outdoors as well. Children enjoy flying kites and roller-skating. Country children like swimming in the rivers. City children go to street libraries, where they can sit and read.

Indoor fun for young people may include movies and Western-style dances. At home, families listen to the radio and play music. Sometimes people gather in a public place to watch TV, but in recent years more and more families have their own set at home.

Chinese people follow many traditions. The New Year Festival is in late January or early February. Fireworks, parades, special foods, and red decorations are part of the New Year celebration.

Steep hillsides are terraced to make flat land for farming and to prevent runoff.

At Guangzhou the fields stretch right up to the very edge of the city.

Sugarcane is grown near Guilin, in sight of the famous limestone hills.

Tea pickers take only the top leaves from the bushes for the tea harvest.

Farming

Most Chinese people are farmers. They grow many kinds of crops, but the main crop is grain. Wheat is grown in the north, and rice is grown in flooded fields in the south. Tea is farmed in hilly areas of central and southern China. Most Chinese farmers grow vegetables and raise chickens and pigs for the family to, eat or sell. Some farmers make ponds to breed fish, if there is no nearby lake or sea.

Farmers live in villages or small towns, unlike farmers in the United States, who have usually lived next to their fields. Until recently Chinese farmers were organized in communes, or groups of people who shared the farm work and profits. Today farm families rent their land at low cost from the government. Important crops, such as grains, must be sold to the government at a price that the government decides. Other crops can be sold for whatever price the farmer can get.

Farmers do the same kind of work in China as farmers do in other parts of the world – they plow, plant, tend, and harvest. However, in China, much of the work is still done by people and animals rather than by machines. In recent years, a small, two-wheeled walking tractor, somewhat like a power lawnmower, has become more common.

Industry

Heavy industry is important in China. There are many coal mines producing fuel for homes and businesses. Factories in central and northeastern China make iron and steel. Other factories produce chemicals, machinery, and clothing.

Most factories and large stores are owned and run by the government. Recently the government has encouraged some people to start their own small businesses, such as cafes and beauty shops.

Tens of millions of Chinese people work in offices. Most of them work for the government. Doctors, teachers, and scientists work for the government, too.

Much of the equipment in factories, stores, and offices is out of date. The Chinese government is trying to change that. Some office work has been difficult because of the nature of the Chinese language. Typewriters were very hard to use. Much of the work had to be copied by hand. One day computers will change all this.

Every worker belongs to a work unit. The work unit arranges many things in life, such as where a family will live and where children will go to school.

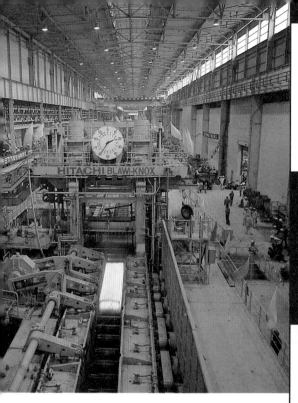

Steel is made in factories like this one in Wuhan. The hot steel glows red as it comes out of the furnace.

This young man is learning the skills that will help him to become an electrical engineer in the future.

Engines like these are made on assembly lines and used in buses, trucks, and tractors.

Famous Landmarks

The Great Wall of China, which extends about 1,500 miles across the north, can be seen from the moon. It was built 2,000 years ago to keep attackers out.

The main shopping street in Shanghai.

The Potala Palace in Lhasa, Tibet.

The terracotta warriors are an army of clay figures made over 2,000 years ago.

The Hall of Prayer in the Temple of Heaven, Beijing.

The Forbidden City, Beijing.

New Year celebration.

Facts and Figures

China—the Land and People

Population:	about 1,152,000,000
Area:	3,691,502 sq. mi.
Length north-south:	about 1,860 mi.
Width east-west:	about 2,000 mi.
Capital city: population:	Beijing (Peking) about 5,800,000
Language:	Mandarin Chinese, with many local variations
Religion:	Confucianism, Buddhism, and Taoism
Money:	Yuan 1 Yuan = 100 Fen
Highest Mountain:	Everest 29,028 feet

Some Chinese Characters

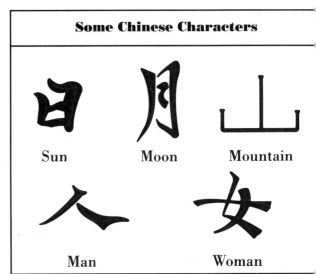

Sun   Moon   Mountain

Man   Woman

Important Dates in Chinese History

c. 1766 BC	Shang dynasty
206 BC – AD 221	Han dynasty
221-581	wars and invasions
581-617	Sui dynasty
617-907	Tang dynasty
907-960	five short dynasties
960-1279	Song dynasty
1279-1368	Yuan dynasty
1368-1644	Ming dynasty
1644-1912	Qing dynasty. The last emperor of China.
1912	Sun Yat-sen elected as the first president.
1937-1945	War with Japan
1945-1949	Civil War between Communists and Nationalists.
1949	People's Republic of China founded by Mao Tse-tung.
1971	China joined the U.N.
1976	Mao dies; later replaced by Deng Xiaoping.
1989	Revolt against old–style communism crushed by tanks.

Average Temperatures in Fahrenheit

	January	June
Shenyang (north)	23°F	86°F
Tianjin (center)	34°F	81°F
Hangzhou (south)	41°F	95°F

Further Reading

Fiction

Ai-Ling, Louie, retold by. *Yeh-Shen: A Cinderella Story from China*. Putnam, 1988

Heyer, Marilee. *The Weaving of a Dream: A Chinese Folktale*. Viking, 1986

Kendall, Carol. *The Wedding of the Rat Family*. Macmillan, 1988

Li, Xiao M., translated from the Chinese. *The Mending of the Sky and Other Chinese Myths*. Oyster River, 1989

Tan, Amy. *The Moon Lady*. Macmillan, 1992

Yep, Laurence. *The Rainbow People*. HarperCollins, 1989

Nonfiction

Ashabranner, Brent. *Land of Yesterday, Land of Tomorrow: Discovering Chinese Central Asia*. Cobblehill/Dutton, 1992

Bright, Michael. *Giant Panda*. Aladdin, 1989

Jacobsen, Karen. *China*. Childrens Press, 1990

Jacobsen, Peter Ott and Preben Sejer Kristensen. *A Family in China*. Watts, 1986

Kalman, Bobbie. *Tibet*. Crabtree, 1990

Thomson, Peggy. *City Kids in China*. HarperCollins, 1993

Waterlow, Julia. *China*. Bookwright, 1990

Wong, Ovid K. *Giant Pandas*. Childrens, 1988

Audiovisuals

Audiocassettes

The Hubei Song and Dance Ensemble of the People's Republic of China—The Imperial Bells of China. Fortuna.

Hung, Lui, with Chinese Orchestra. *Chinese Folk Songs*. Lyrichord.

S. McKenna. *Chinese Fairy Tales*. Caedmon.

Videotapes

The China Series. Ambrose Video Publishing, Inc. 1988

Chinese New Years. Spoken Arts, Inc., 1991

They Sing—We Sing Chinese. Film Ideas, Inc., 1989

Index

© 1993 Globe Enterprises